HAL•LEONARD

GUITAR PLAY-ALONG

VOL. 175

MICHAEL SCHENKER

M000159701

CONTENTS

Cover photo © Pete Cronin/Redferns

ISBN 978-1-4803-5421-0

HAL•LEONARD®
CORPORATION

7777 W. BLUEMOUND RD. P.O. BOX 13819 MILWAUKEE, WI 53213

In Australia Contact:
Hal Leonard Australia Pty. Ltd.
4 Lentara Court
Cheltenham, Victoria, 3192 Australia
Email: ausadmin@halleonard.com.au

Visit Hal Leonard Online at
www.halleonard.com

Armed and Ready

Words and Music by Michael Schenker and Gary Barden

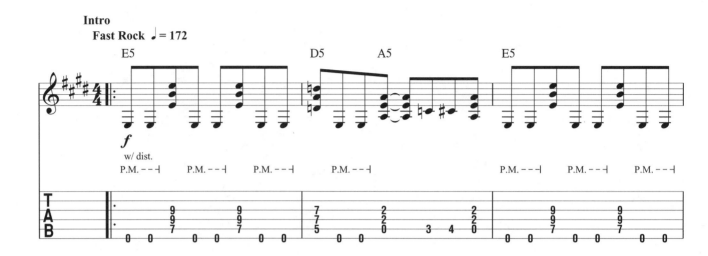

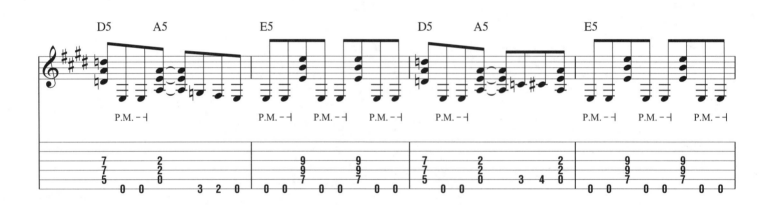

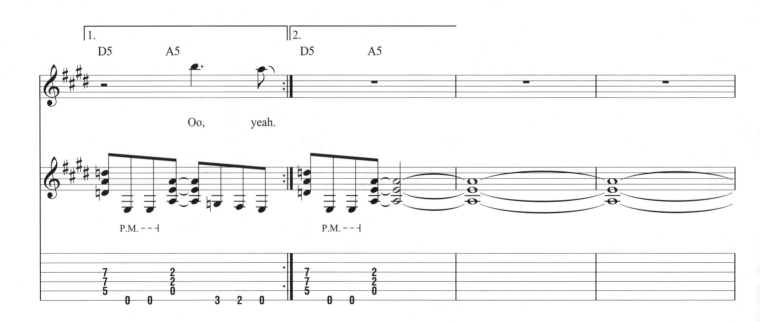

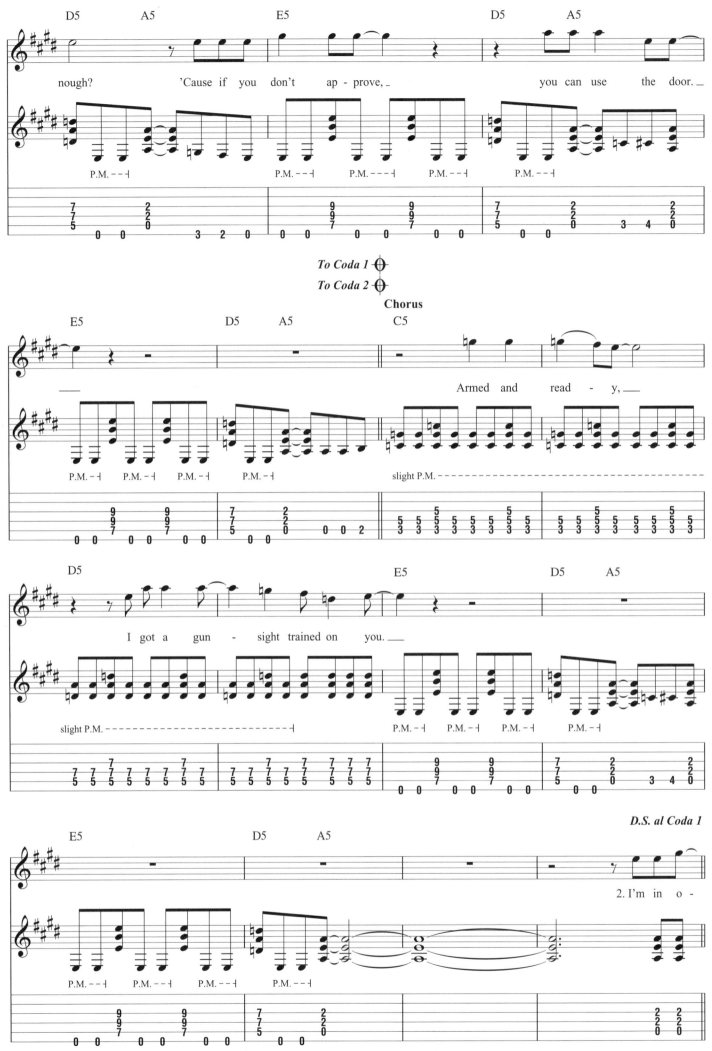

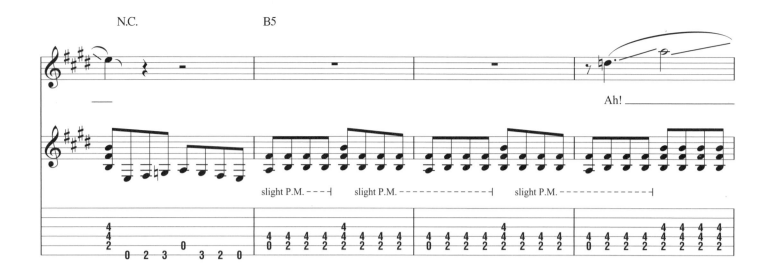

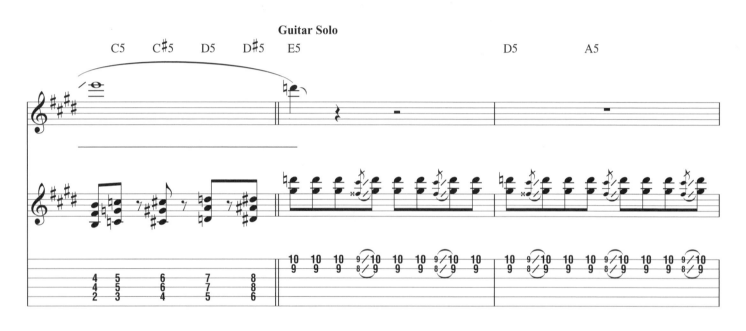

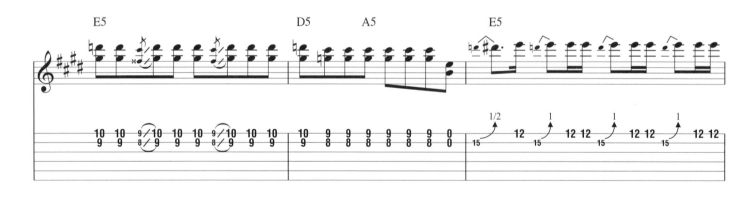

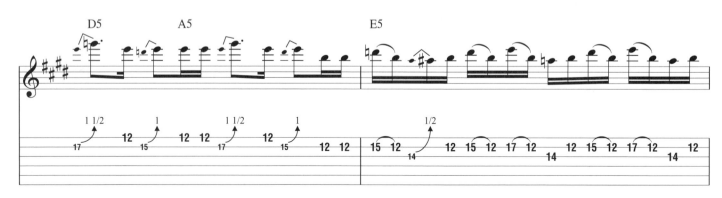

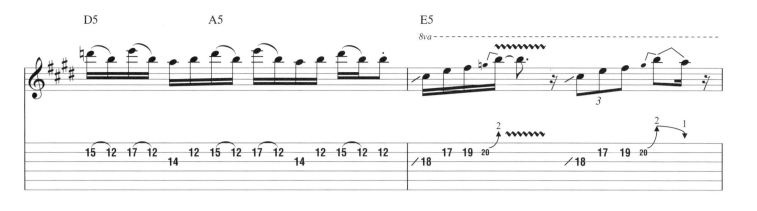

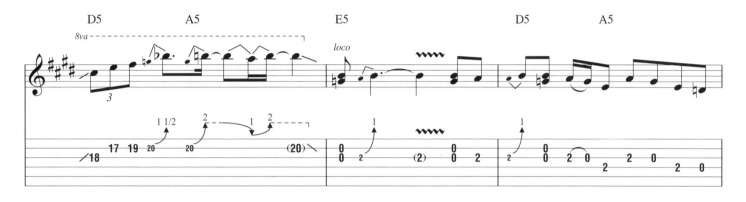

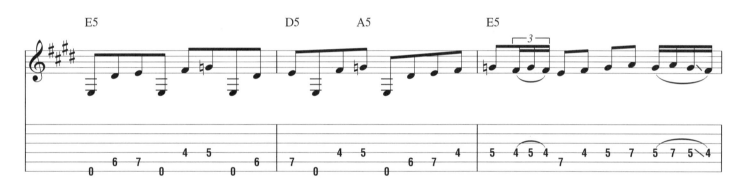

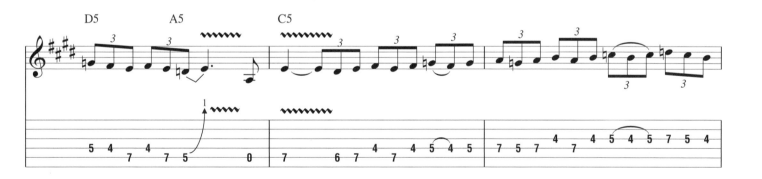

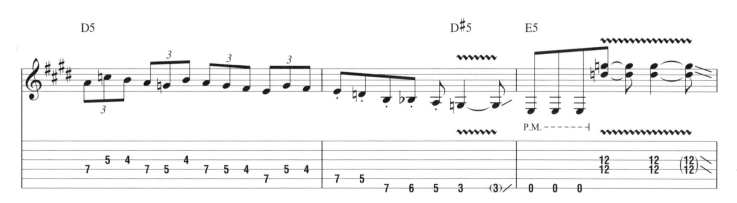

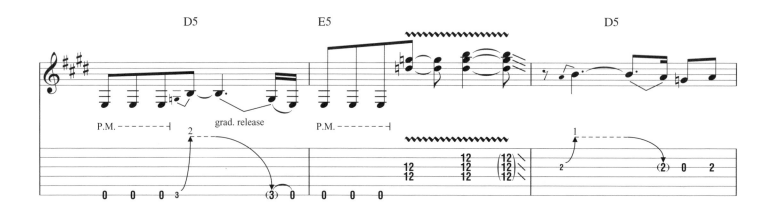

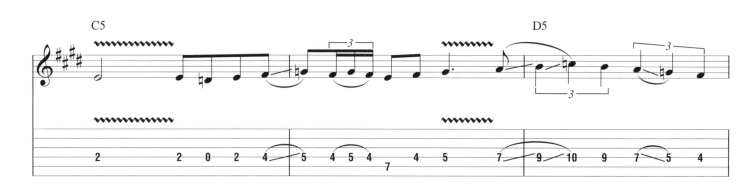

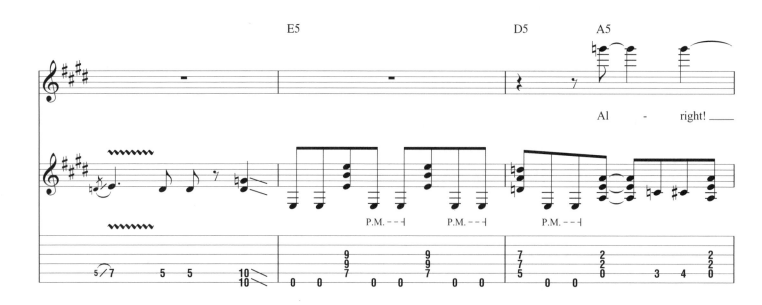

D.S. al Coda 2

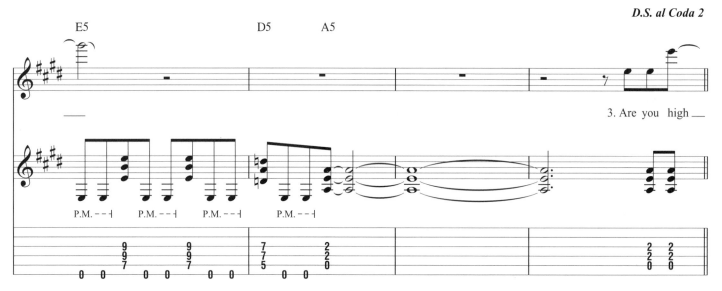

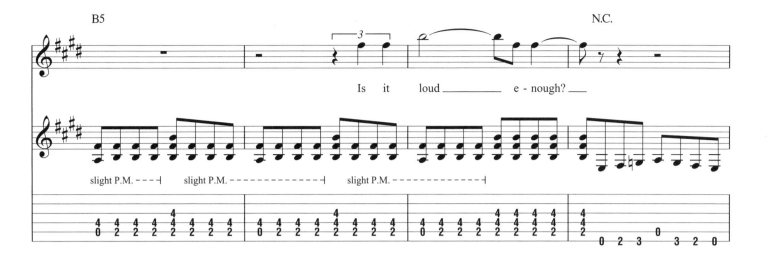

Is it loud _____ e - nough? _____

slight P.M. - - - -   slight P.M. - - - - - - - - - - - -   slight P.M. - - - - - - - - - - - -

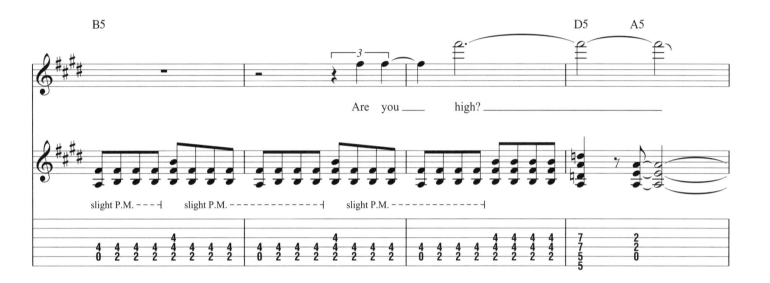

Are you _____ high? _____

slight P.M. - - - -   slight P.M. - - - - - - - - - - - -   slight P.M. - - - - - - - - - - - -

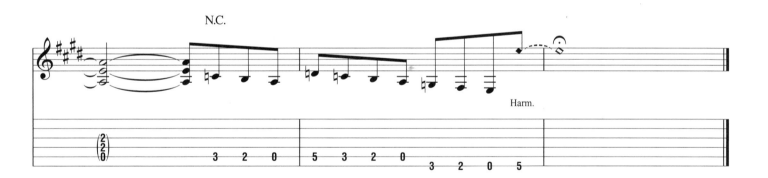

Harm.

Additional Lyrics

2. I'm in overdrive, and I feel alive, oh.
   Got ev'rything I need and that ain't all.
   Got a thing to do, I wanna do for you.
   I wanna see you jump like hell when I call.

3. Are you high tonight? Are you feelin' right?
   'Cause I need you now like I never did before.
   Is it hard enough? Is it loud enough?
   And if you don't approve, use the door.

Captain Nemo

By Michael Schenker

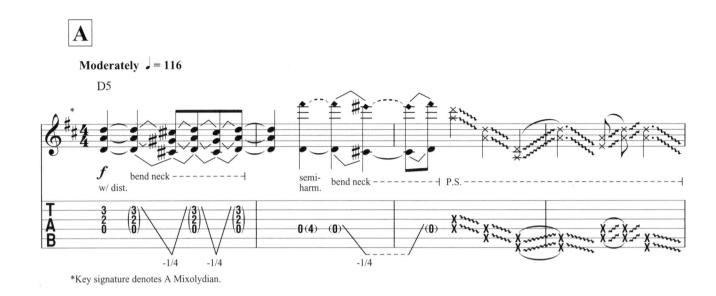

*Key signature denotes A Mixolydian.

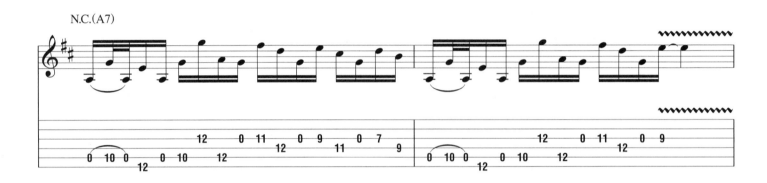

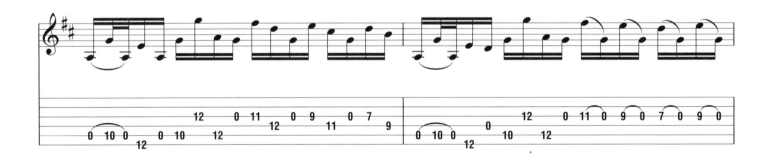

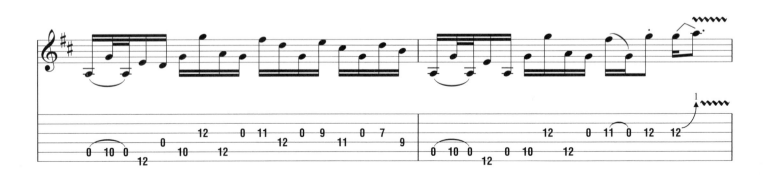

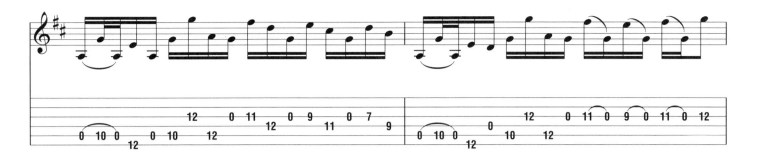

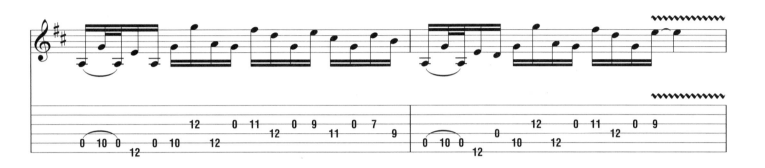

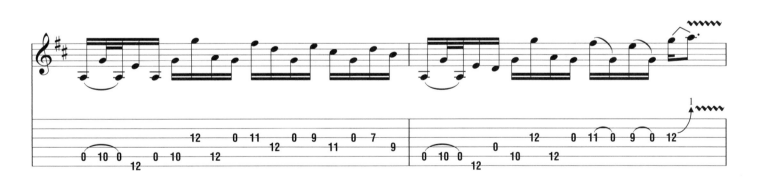

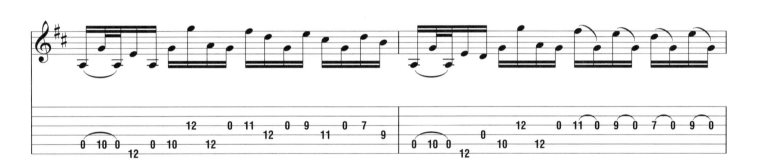

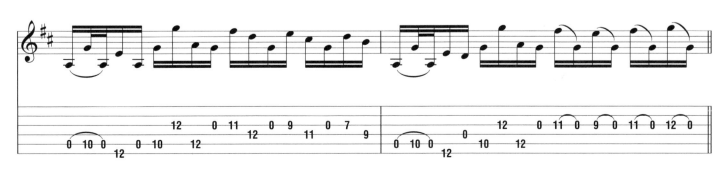

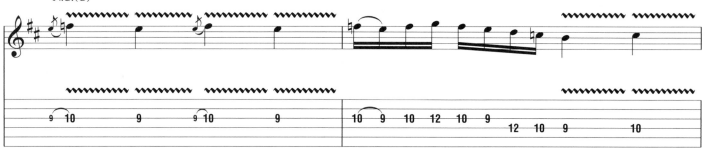

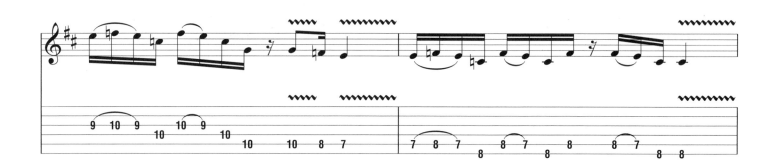

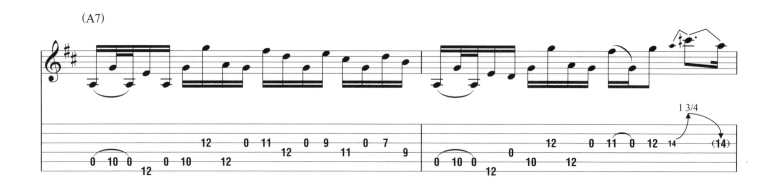

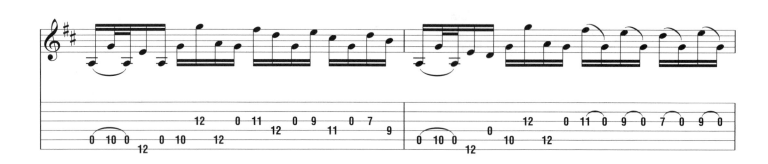

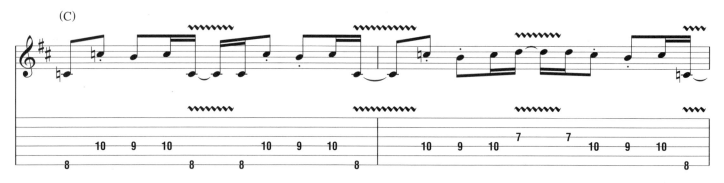

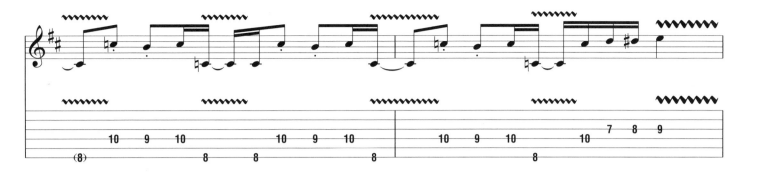

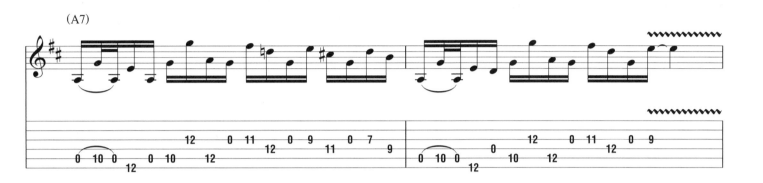

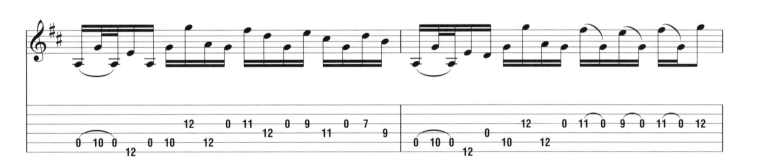

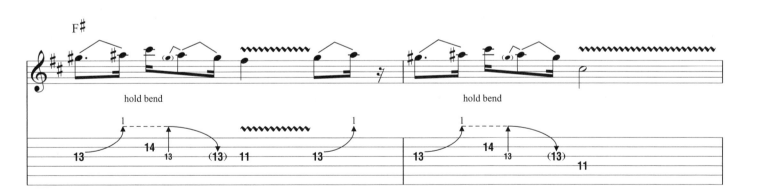

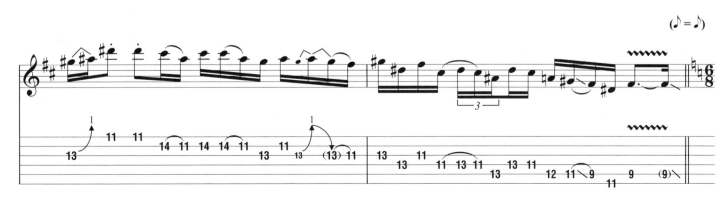

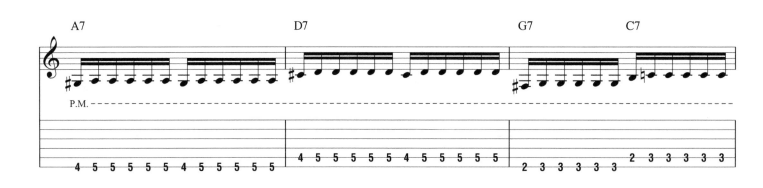

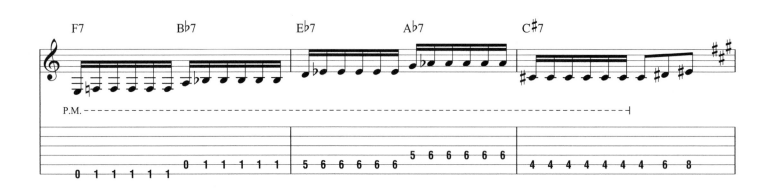

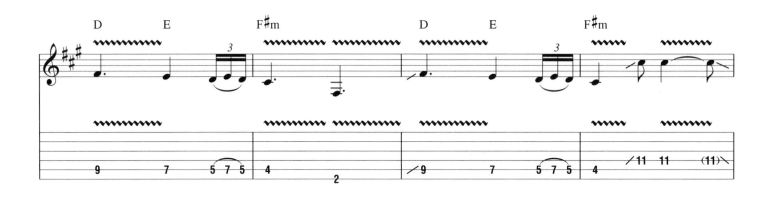

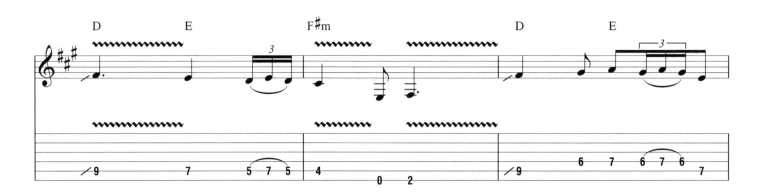

Doctor, Doctor

Words and Music by Michael Schenker and Phillip Mogg

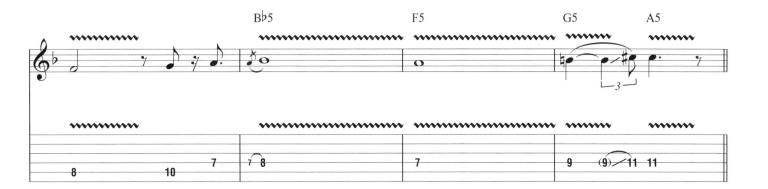

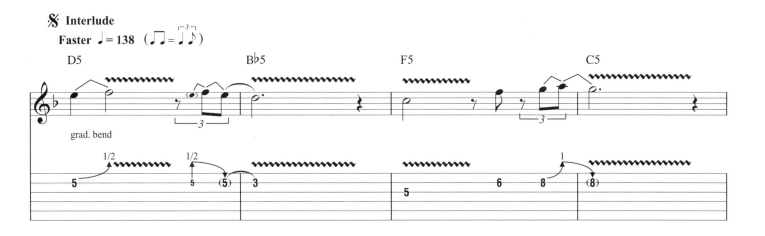

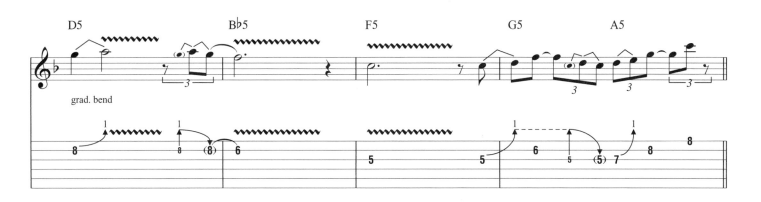

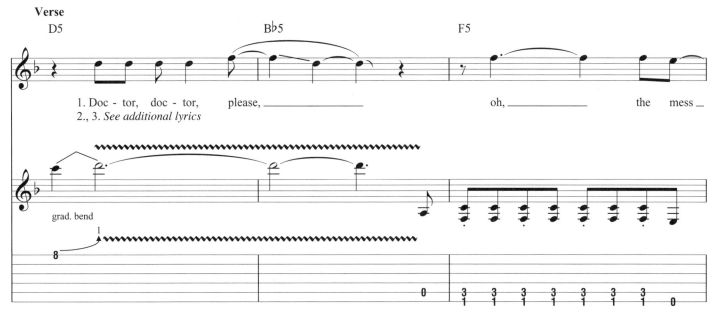

Outro

Additional Lyrics

2. Doctor, doctor, please, oh, I'm goin' fast.
   Doctor, doctor, please, oh, I'm goin' fast.
   It's only just a moment, she's turnin' paranoid.
   That's not a situation for a n-nervous boy.

3. Doctor, doctor, please, oh, the mess I'm in.
   Doctor, doctor, please, oh, the mess I'm in.
   But you looked so angry as I crawled across your floor.
   She's got the strain, and I can't take any more.

Into the Arena

By Michael Schenker

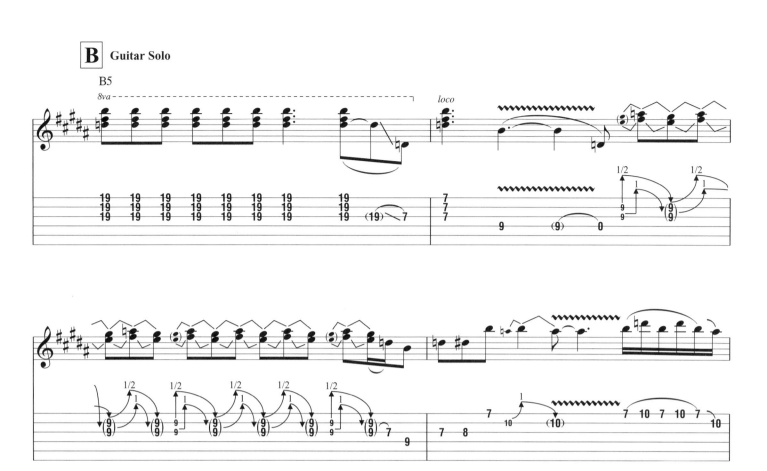

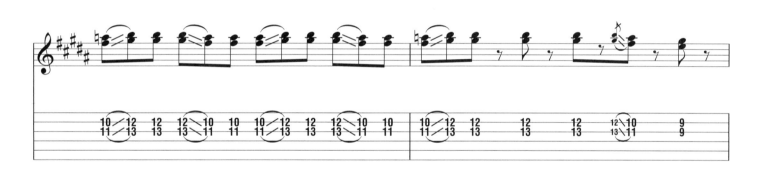

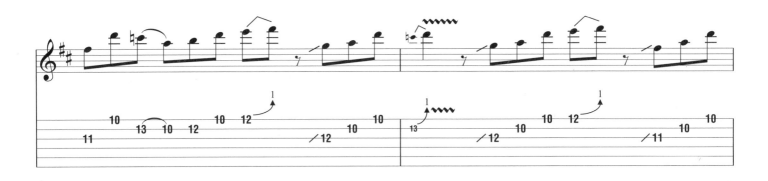

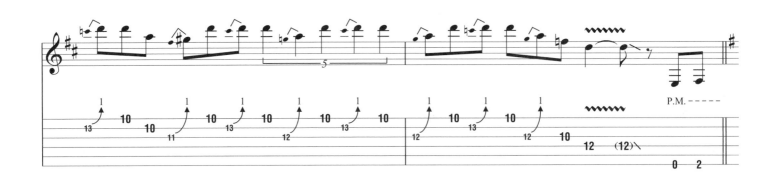

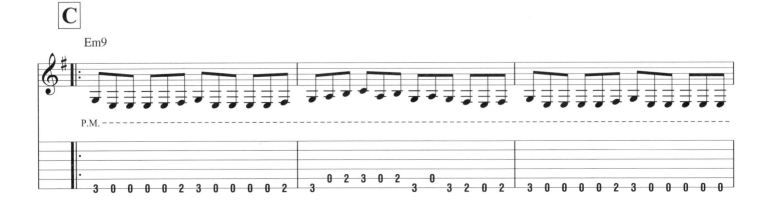

C

Em9

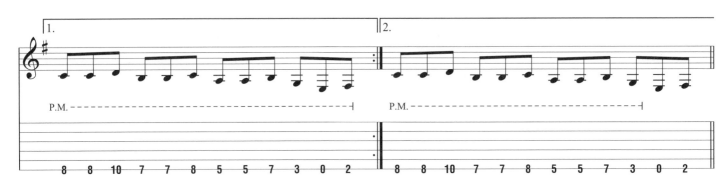

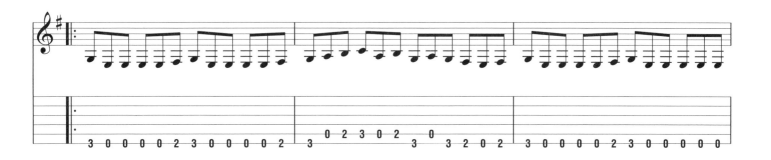

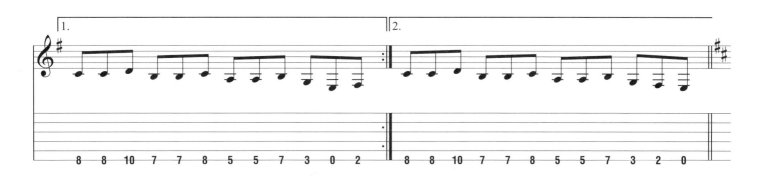

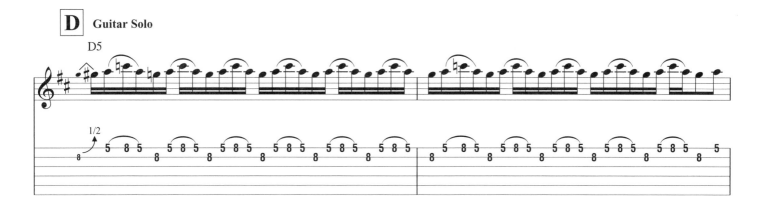

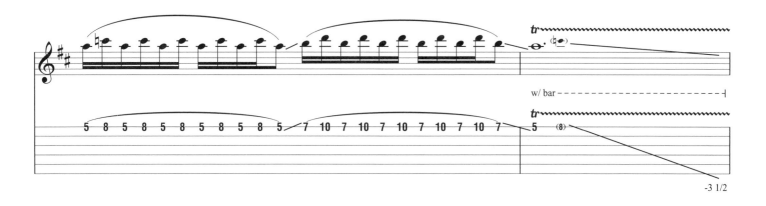

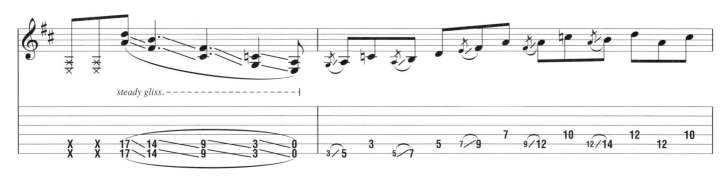

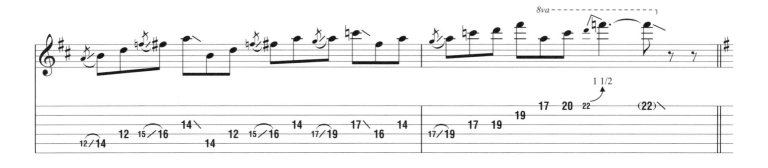

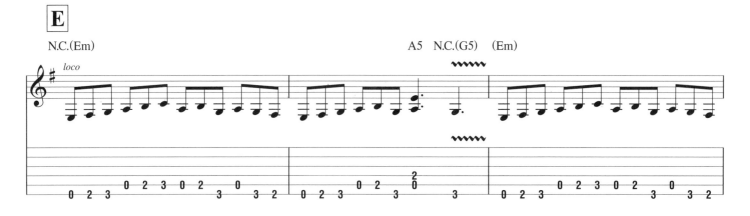

E

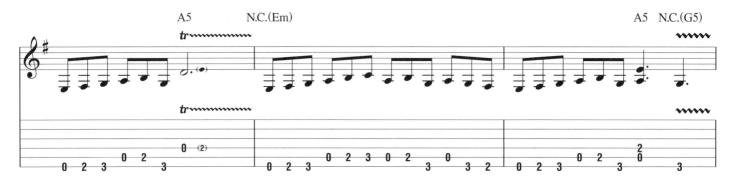

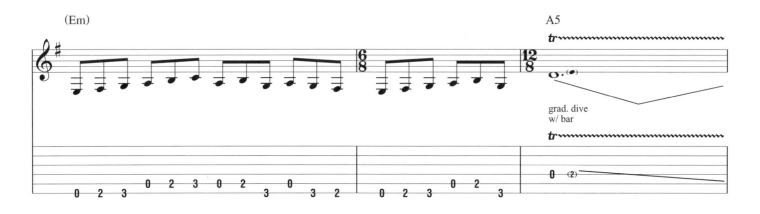

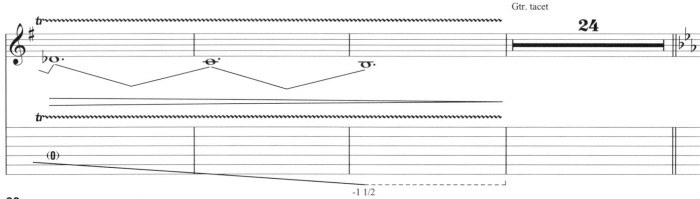

Lights Out

Words and Music by Michael Schenker, Phil Mogg, Andy Parker and Pete Way

Intro
Moderately fast Rock ♩ = 152

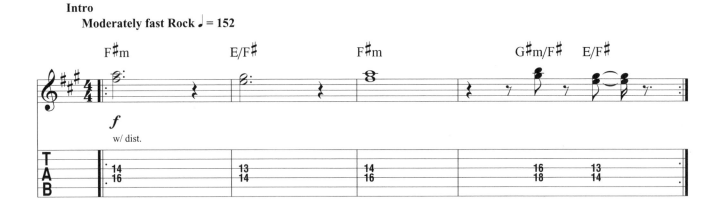

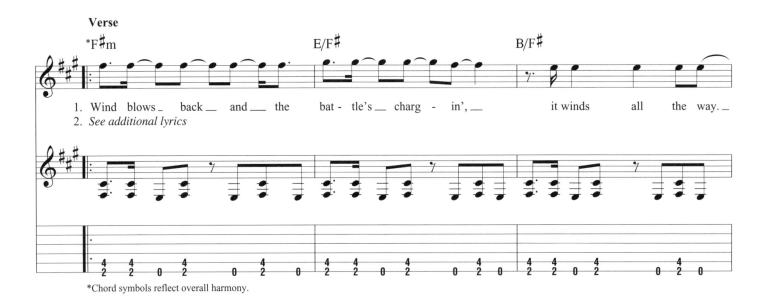

1. Wind blows back and the bat-tle's charg-in', it winds all the way.
2. *See additional lyrics*

*Chord symbols reflect overall harmony.

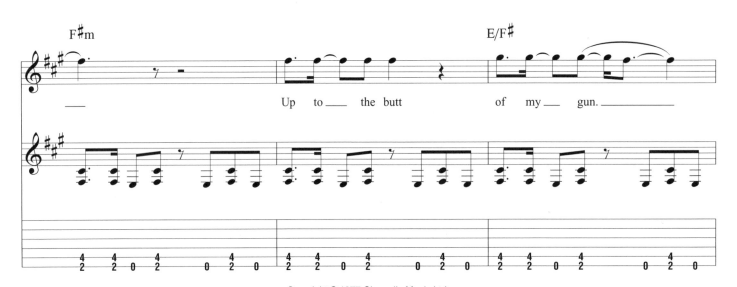

Up to the butt of my gun.

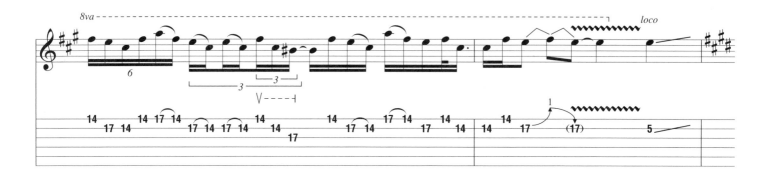

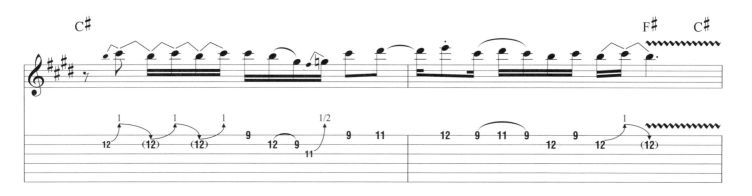

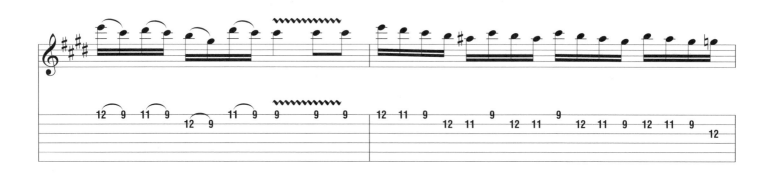

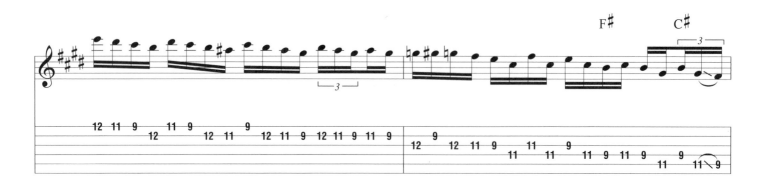

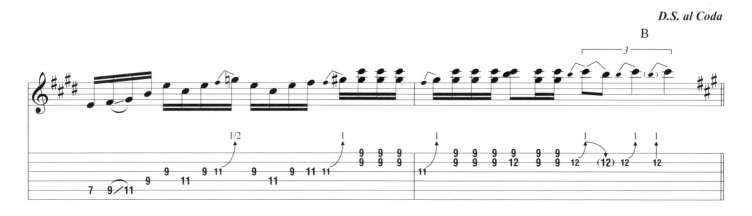

Outro-Guitar Solo

Lights out, lights __ out __ in Lon - don.

Begin fade

Lights out, lights _____ out _____ in Lon - don.

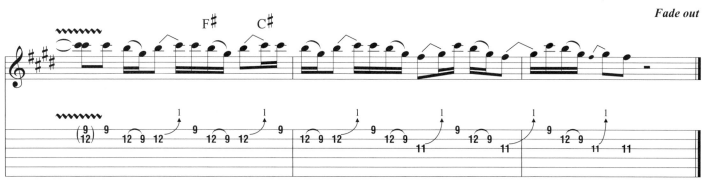

Fade out

Additional Lyrics

2. From the back streets
   There's a rumblin';
   Smell of anarchy.
   No more nice time,
   Bright boy shoe shines;
   Pie-in-the-sky dreams.

4. You keep comin',
   There's no runnin';
   Tried a thousand times.
   Under your feet,
   Grass is growin'.
   Time we said goodbye.

On and On

Words and Music by Michael Schenker and Gary Barden

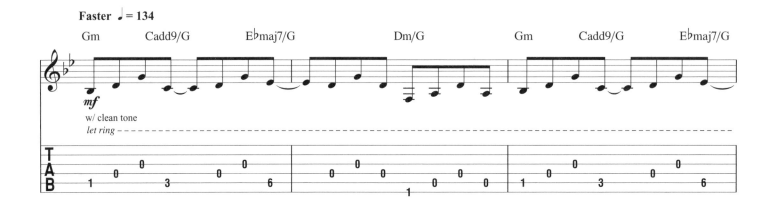

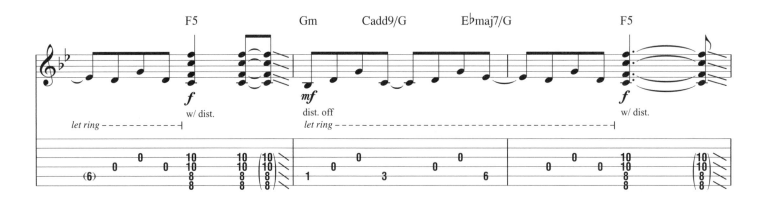

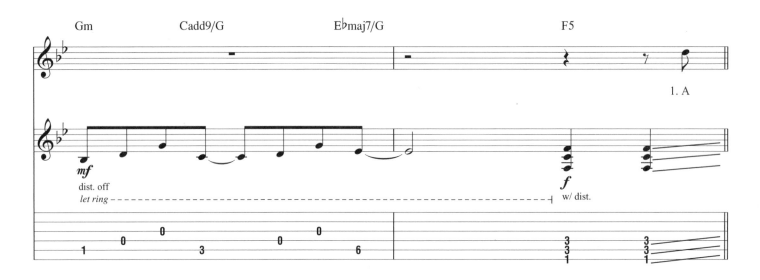

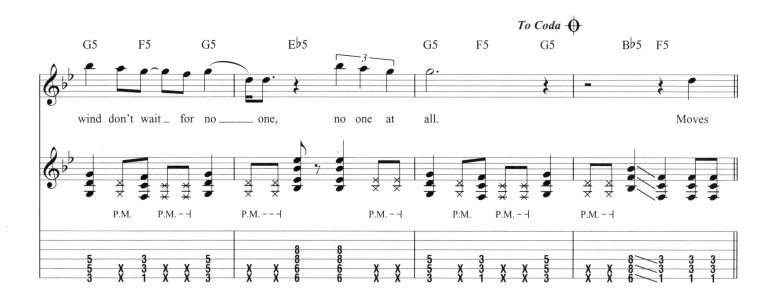

wind don't wait _ for no _____ one, no one at all. Moves

Chorus

on and on ____ and on ____ and on ____ and on. ____

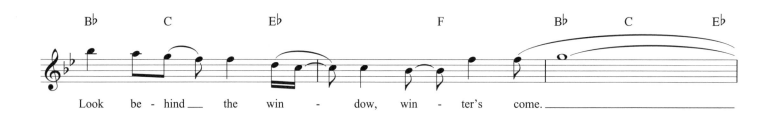

Look be - hind ___ the win - dow, win - ter's come. _____

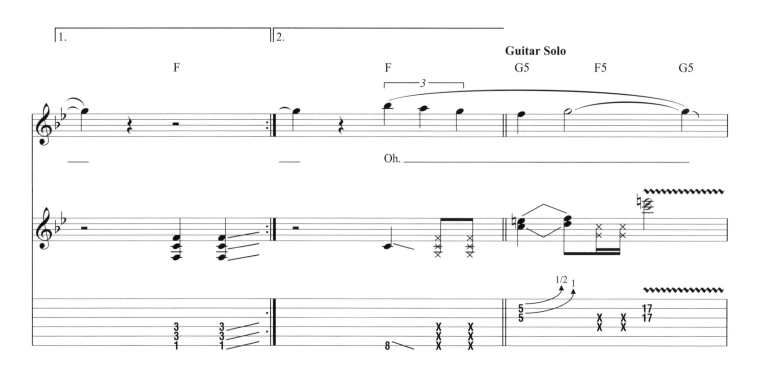

____ ____ Oh. _____

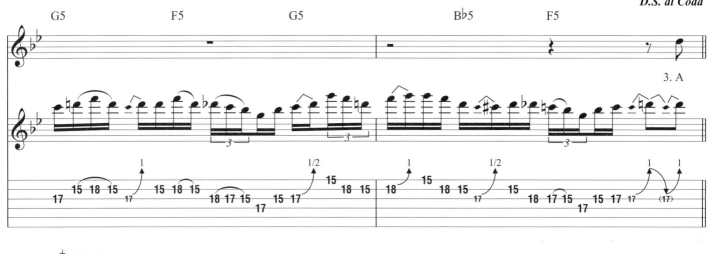

Look be - hind, the wind is com - in' now. _____

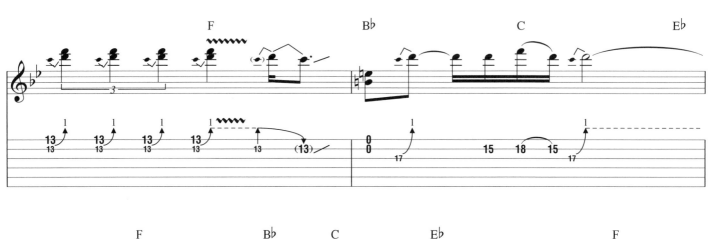

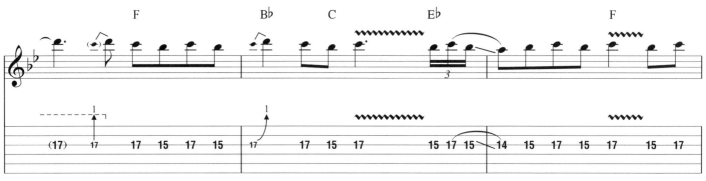

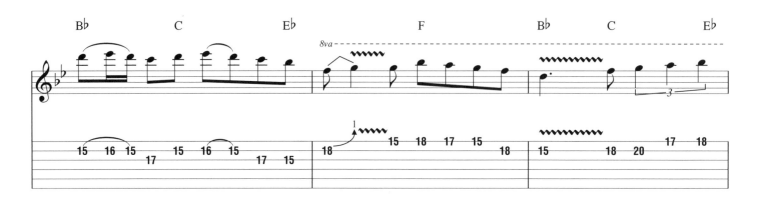

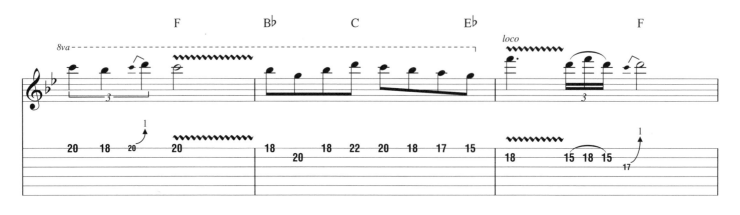

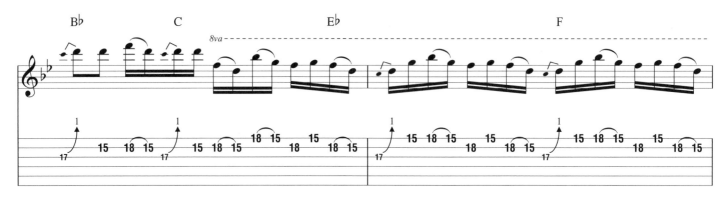

Additional Lyrics

2. Blood on the streets when the black skies shout and the people cry no more.
Dreams just fade away, reality soars.
His crime is his fate, can't think, can't relate, illusion's seized his mind.
Key to all the answers are locked in his eyes.

Rock Bottom

Words and Music by Michael Schenker and Phillip Mogg

Chorus

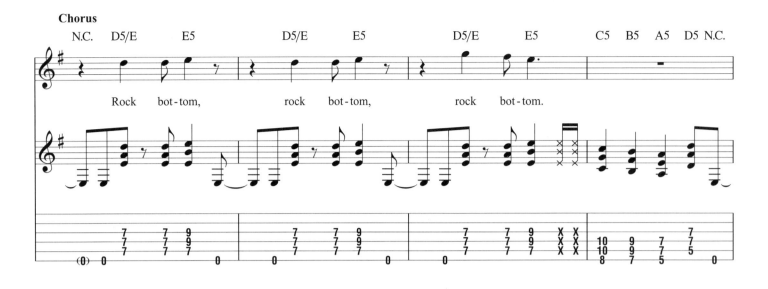

Rock bot-tom, rock bot-tom, rock bot-tom.

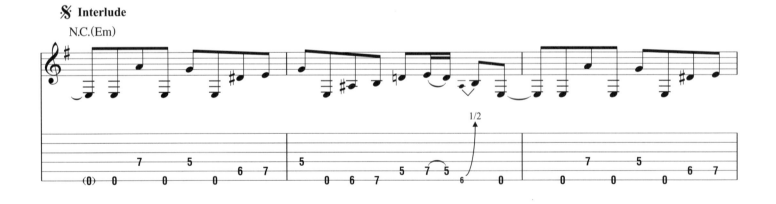

To Coda ⊕

Rock bot-tom, rock bot-tom, rock bot-tom.

𝄋 **Interlude**

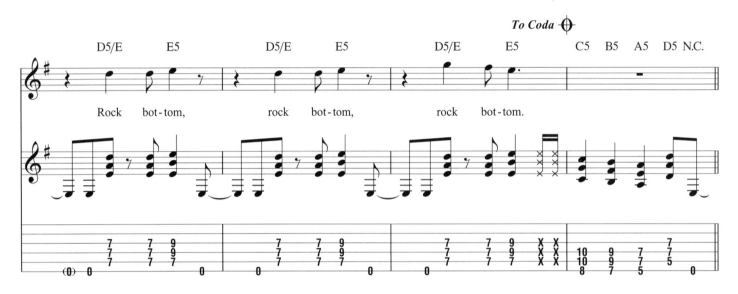

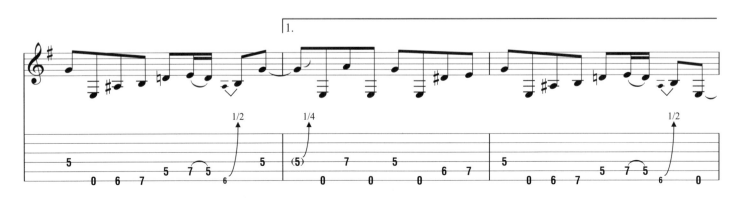

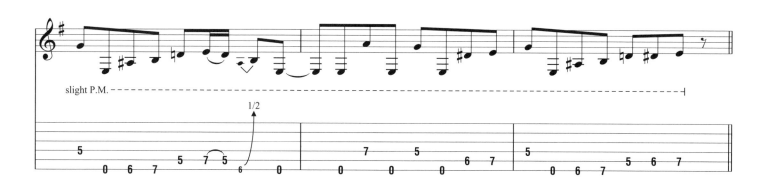

Bridge
Half-time feel

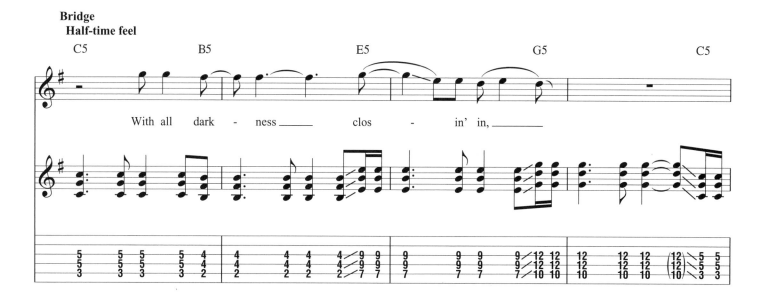

With all dark - ness _____ clos - in' in, _____

will the light __ re - veal __ your soul?

End half-time feel

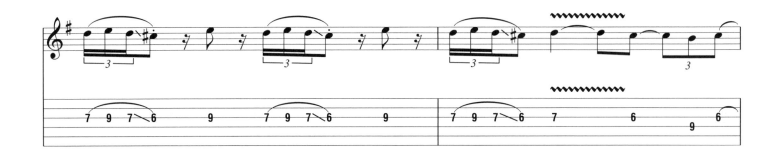

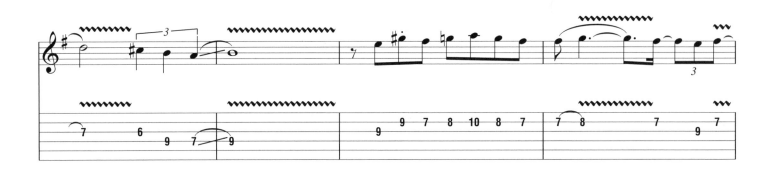

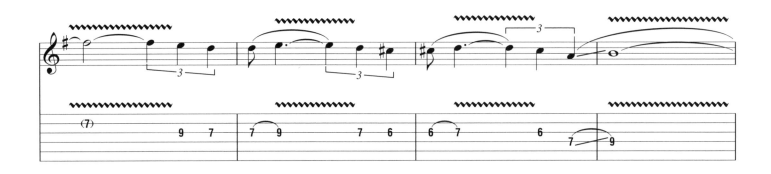

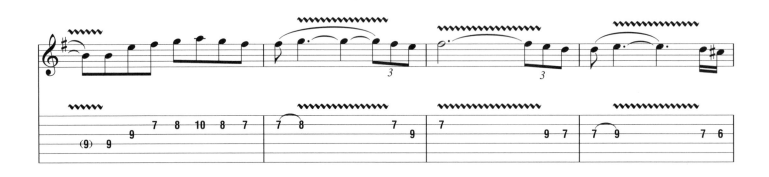

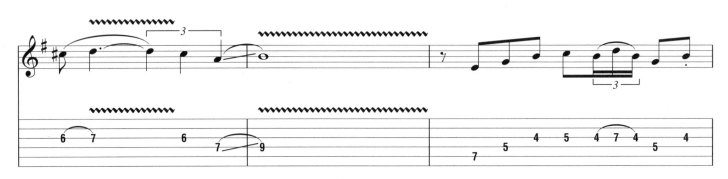

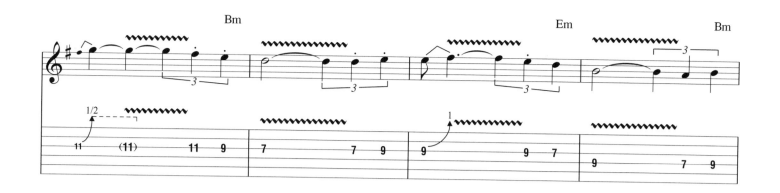

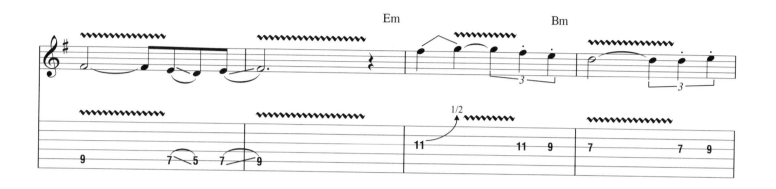

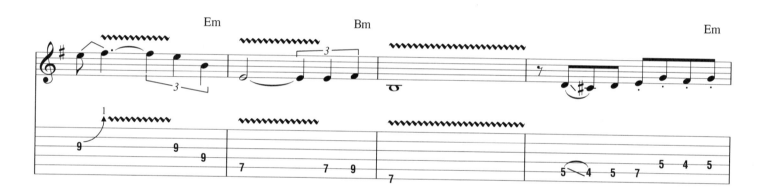

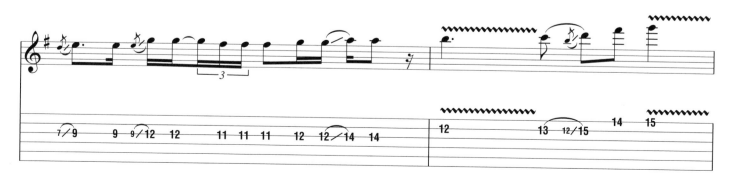

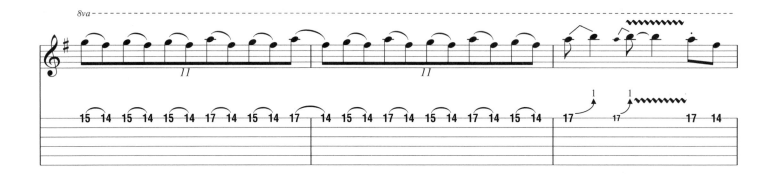

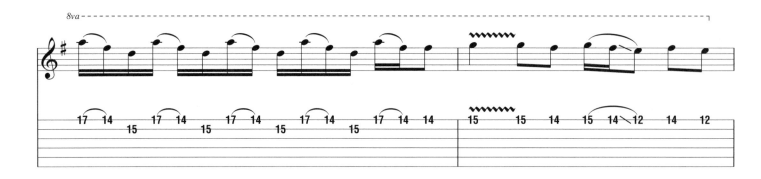

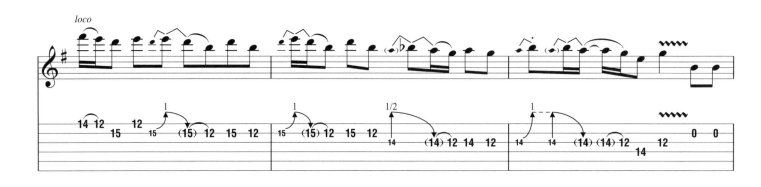

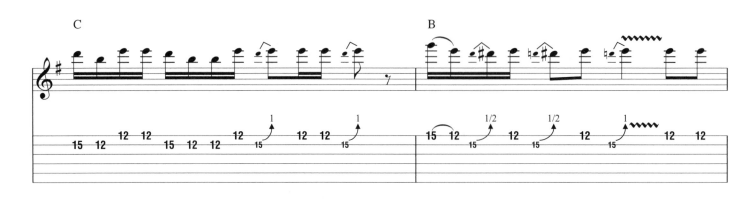

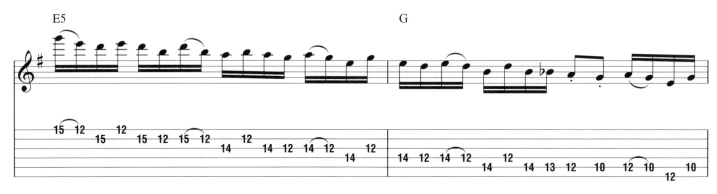

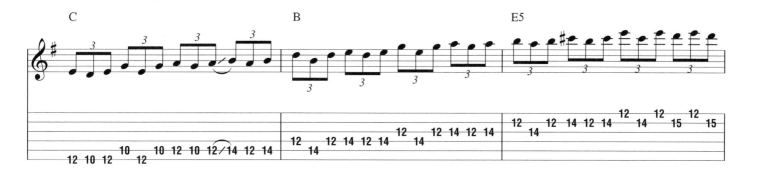

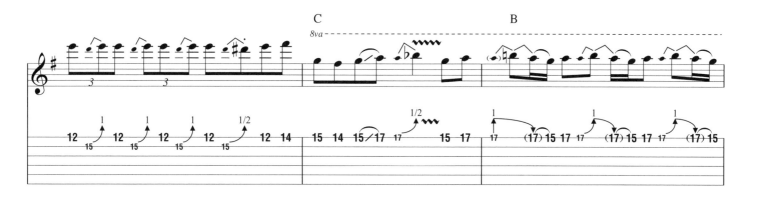

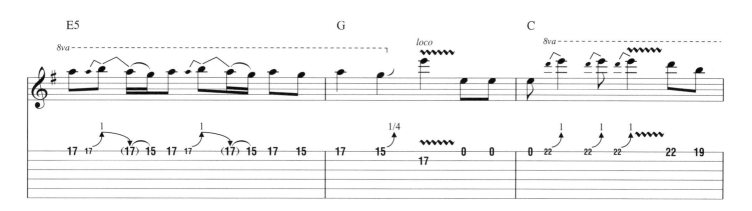

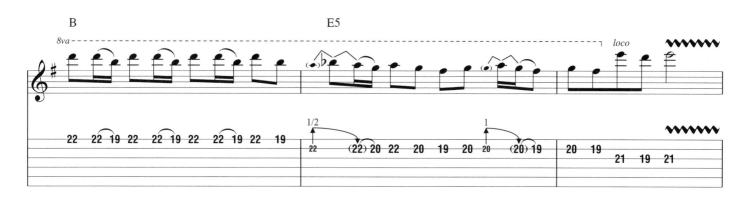

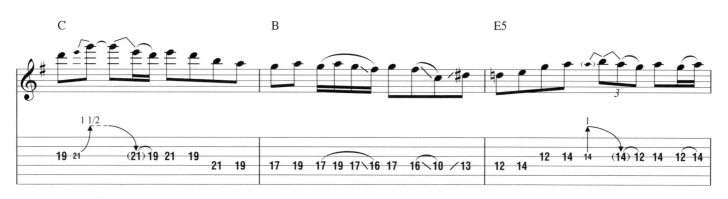

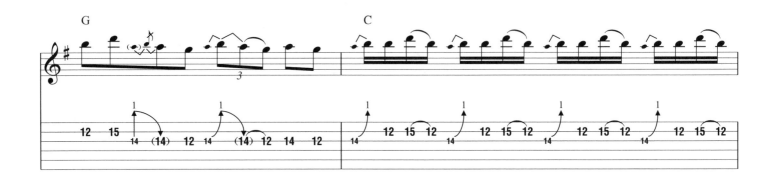

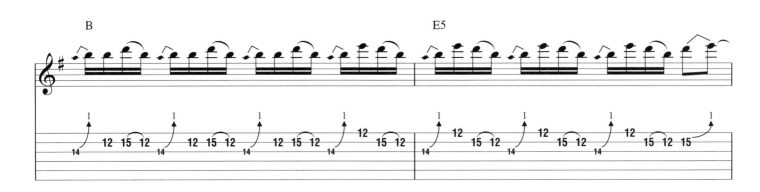

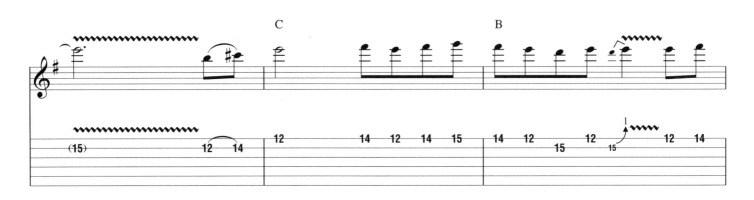

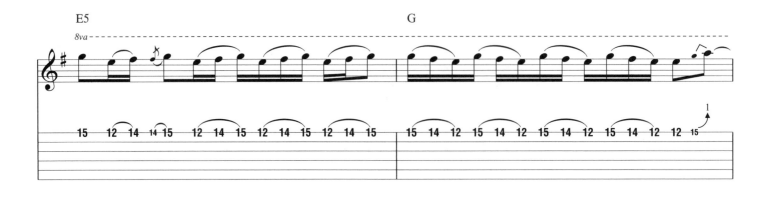

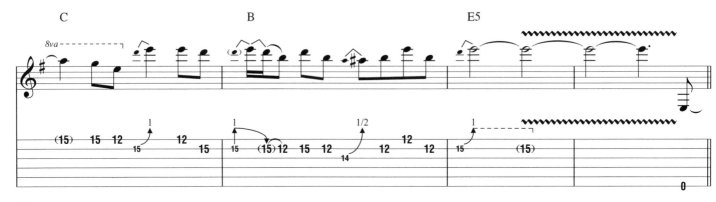

Interlude

⊕ Coda

Outro

Additional Lyrics

2. Shadow Earth is closin' in above the lamps in your street.
   Lucifer goes walkin' down for you to meet.
   Minutes pass so slowly by the hands on your clock.
   Heaven's door, just nowhere and you can't knock.

Too Hot to Handle

Words and Music by Phil Moog and Pete Way

hot, { mm, ___ / ba - by, ___ } too hot ___ to han - dle.

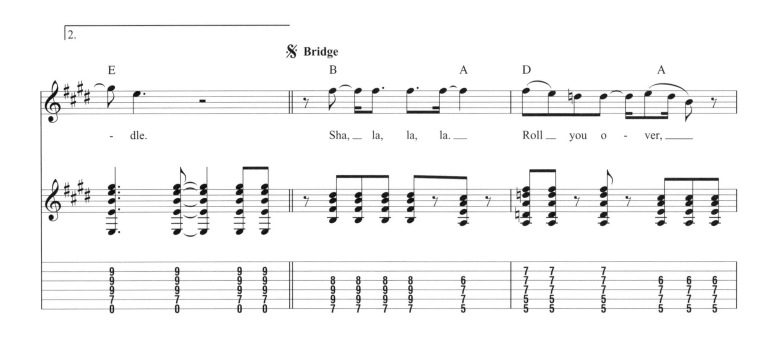

% Bridge

- dle. Sha, ___ la, la, la. ___ Roll ___ you o - ver, ___

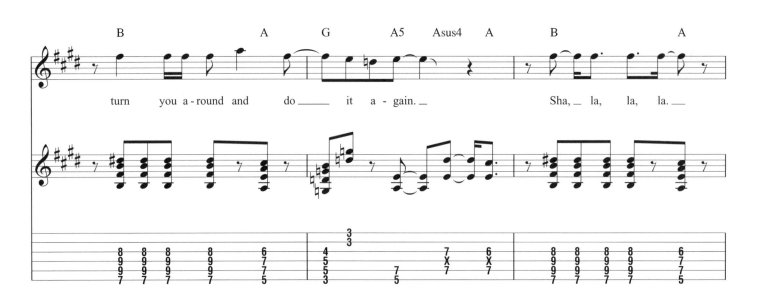

turn you a - round and do ___ it a - gain. ___ Sha, ___ la, la, la. ___

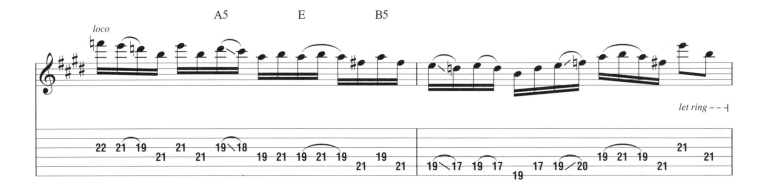

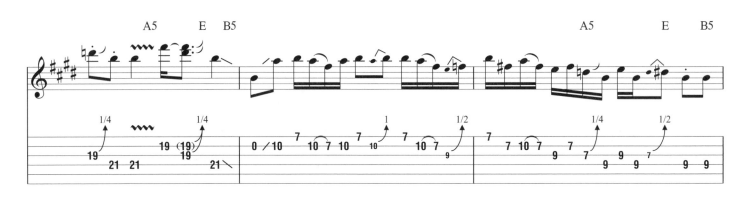

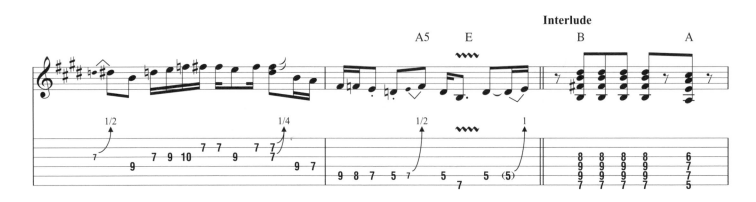

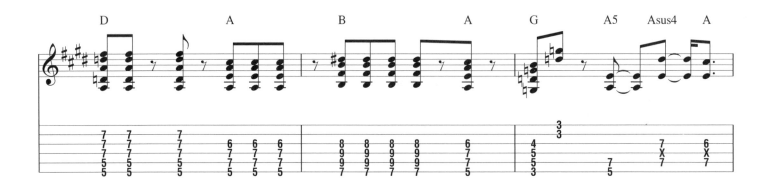

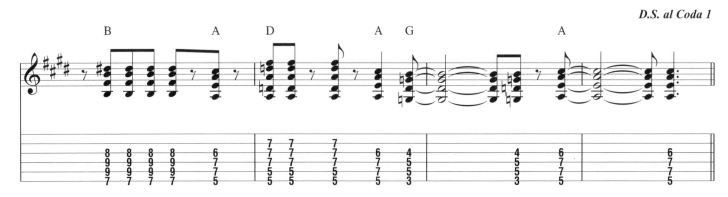

⊕ Coda 1

⊕ Coda 2

Outro-Guitar Solo

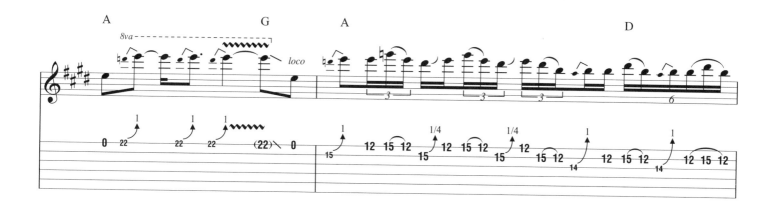

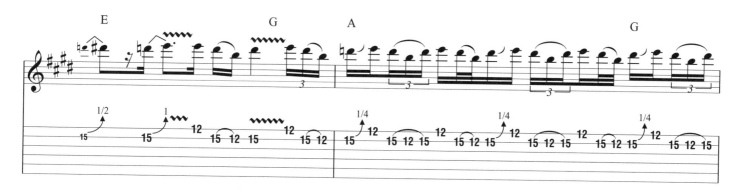

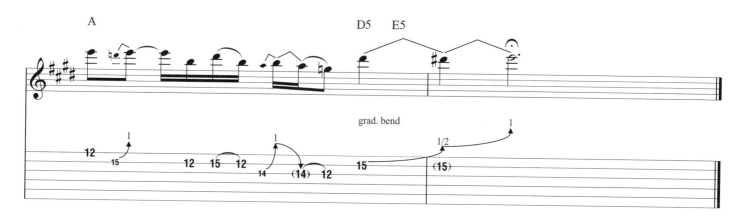

Additional Lyrics

2. Wink of an eye, the feelin's run high,
   A real rock and roll molest.
   But I ain't no romance and I ain't no slow chance.
   Won't get no quick change.

3. I'm in your town, won't fool around.
   I'll make some action stick.
   Just like the story says, these boys are bad,
   So keep out of shootin' range.

GUITAR NOTATION LEGEND

THE MUSICAL STAFF shows pitches and rhythms and is divided by bar lines into measures. Pitches are named after the first seven letters of the alphabet.

TABLATURE graphically represents the guitar fingerboard. Each horizontal line represents a string, and each number represents a fret.

4th string, 2nd fret   1st & 2nd strings open, played together   open D chord

HALF-STEP BEND: Strike the note and bend up 1/2 step.

WHOLE-STEP BEND: Strike the note and bend up one step.

GRACE NOTE BEND: Strike the note and immediately bend up as indicated.

SLIGHT (MICROTONE) BEND: Strike the note and bend up 1/4 step.

BEND AND RELEASE: Strike the note and bend up as indicated, then release back to the original note. Only the first note is struck.

PRE-BEND: Bend the note as indicated, then strike it.

VIBRATO: The string is vibrated by rapidly bending and releasing the note with the fretting hand.

PALM MUTING: The note is partially muted by the pick hand lightly touching the string(s) just before the bridge.

HAMMER-ON: Strike the first (lower) note with one finger, then sound the higher note (on the same string) with another finger by fretting it without picking.

PULL-OFF: Place both fingers on the notes to be sounded. Strike the first note and without picking, pull the finger off to sound the second (lower) note.

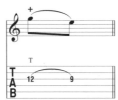

LEGATO SLIDE: Strike the first note and then slide the same fret-hand finger up or down to the second note. The second note is not struck.

SHIFT SLIDE: Same as legato slide, except the second note is struck.

TRILL: Very rapidly alternate between the notes indicated by continuously hammering on and pulling off.

TAPPING: Hammer ("tap") the fret indicated with the pick-hand index or middle finger and pull off to the note fretted by the fret hand.

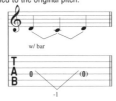

NATURAL HARMONIC: Strike the note while the fret-hand lightly touches the string directly over the fret indicated.

PINCH HARMONIC: The note is fretted normally and a harmonic is produced by adding the edge of the thumb or the tip of the index finger of the pick hand to the normal pick attack.

TREMOLO PICKING: The note is picked as rapidly and continuously as possible.

VIBRATO BAR DIVE AND RETURN: The pitch of the note or chord is dropped a specified number of steps (in rhythm), then returned to the original pitch.

VIBRATO BAR SCOOP: Depress the bar just before striking the note, then quickly release the bar.

VIBRATO BAR DIP: Strike the note and then immediately drop a specified number of steps, then release back to the original pitch.

Additional Musical Definitions

(accent) • Accentuate note (play it louder).

(staccato) • Play the note short.

D.S. al Coda • Go back to the sign (𝄋), then play until the measure marked "*To Coda*," then skip to the section labelled "**Coda**."

D.C. al Fine • Go back to the beginning of the song and play until the measure marked "*Fine*" (end).

Fill • Label used to identify a brief melodic figure which is to be inserted into the arrangement.

N.C. • Harmony is implied.

• Repeat measures between signs.

• When a repeated section has different endings, play the first ending only the first time and the second ending only the second time.